GOD-TALK WITH YOUNG CHILDREN

GOD-TALK
with
YOUNG CHILDREN

Notes for Parents and Teachers

JOHN M. HULL

Trinity Press International
Philadelphia

First Published 1991

Trinity Press International
3725 Chestnut Street
Philadelphia, PA 19104

Cover design: Brian Preuss

Originally published by CEM, Derby, England as Birmingham Papers in Religious Education No. 2, 1991.

Library of Congress Cataloging-in-Publication Data

Hull, John M.
    God-talk with young children : notes for parents and teachers /
  John M. Hull
      p.   cm.
    Includes bibliographical references.
    ISBN 1-56338-028-5 (pbk.)
    1. Christian education of children. 2. God. 3. Children—
  Religious life. 4. Christian education—Home training. I. Title.
  BV1475.H85   1991
  268'.432—dc20
                                                       91-37858
                                                          CIP

CONTENTS

Contents

FOREWORD

One of the most profound images of God that I know—the image is Nelle Morton's—is of God as a Great Listening at the core of the universe, hearing us into speech. Reading John Hull's beautiful little book, I am reminded of this image. For at the book's center is a similar great listening: this time the listening adults can provide children. Such listening hears children not only into speech, but into an exploration of questions about the Bible, morality, prayer, heaven, and earth. Mainly, however, it enables them to pursue questions about God.

Religious educators throughout Great Britain, the Commonwealth countries, and Europe have long known John Hull as one of the preeminent figures in their field. This volume, coming so soon after his masterful *Touching the Rock,* should provide further understanding why this is so to those U.S. readers only beginning to know him. The earlier book, profound in its religious consciousness and luminous in its account of the experience of his blindness, introduced many readers not only to John, but to his children, especially Thomas and Lizzie (whom I had the joy of meeting in Birmingham in 1983). An older Thomas and Lizzie—with their siblings—appear here and anchor us in the reality of children's talk about God.

Whether we are parents or teachers in churches, temples, or public schools, those of us who pick up this volume should find it especially valuable in allowing us to enter three realms with the children in our care: the realms of *conversation, imagination,* and *teaching.* To help us dwell with children in the realm of *conversation,* Hull gives theoretical grounding on the structure of conversation itself. His delineation of five stages of conversation, preceded by an early period of what can be called "pre-argumentation," clarifies what goes on as children grow in their capacities to articulate what they are thinking. His reflection on conversational intervention as a technique for teachers and parents is also helpful and provocative.

But the core of his contribution lies in concrete and particular accounts of actual conversations between him and his children in the safe environment where the children obviously know someone who cares is listening. From the perspective of the adult interlocutor, these conversations take the children seriously, do not violate their tentative searchings, and come across as based on a conviction of a child's right to be heard and trusted to discover her or his own answers to religious questions. They are also marvelously laced with humor and wit on the part of the adult, and delight and merriment on the part of the child. Commenting on the entire enterprise at one point, Hull makes the wise observation that often, in talking over religious questions, the satisfying thing for children is the conversation itself. Eventually, as Rilke noted, they live along into the answers that emerge.

The second realm to which this book invites is *imagination*. Actually, the book might be described as a book about religious imagination, and even more precisely as about religious images: about the richness of children's imagery, and about the ways adults can facilitate the development of such imagery. John Hull insists that children develop as extensive a repertoire of images of God as possible, and laments the paucity of God-images too often limiting their religious imaginations. In fact, he asserts it is better for children to have too many images of the divine than too few. Whether these come from Nordic myth, Hebrew Bible, or the natural world, all are grist for milling understandings of God. Perhaps it is even true that to know only one image of God is to know none. At any rate, the contribution adults can make lies in following the lead of the child in image-making, encouraging the pursuit, and confirming and extending the images discovered.

The way this is done is through a particular mode of *teaching*, extensively modeled throughout the book. Hull makes it clear that no child asks a question without experiencing a difficulty or being challenged by a problem. Therefore the teaching role is to listen to these questions, to feed these back or rephrase them, but only rarely to give precise answers. As a teacher of teachers, I can envision asking adult students of teaching to take the conversations presented in this book, to study and contemplate them, and to try to understand how, when, and where they might replicate similar ones. Such an exercise could make it possible for adults, whether in parental or instructional roles, to assist children to enter the mystery of God. And that, in turn, might open up what Hull refers to as a "rich vein of human experience and spiritual sensitivity" where adults find they are not only teaching children but learning from them as well. Such, I hope and I predict, will be only one of the many rewards awaiting readers of *God-Talk with Young Children.*

Maria Harris
Visiting Professor of Religious Education
Fordham University
August 1991

INTRODUCTION

Several concerns have led to this study of children's conversations about God. There is, first of all, a problem in the religious education of young children in county schools. There is often a tendency to concentrate upon preliminaries and a reluctance to teach children about the central issues of religion. The result is that many children are not acquiring the vocabulary which will enable them to talk about God and the issues of human life which God-talk entails. This is a loss not only to the religious education of the children but to their general social, personal, and cultural development.

There are many factors in this reluctance to teach children how to talk about God, but one central issue is the fact that many teachers believe that young children are incapable of such conversation. My experience, and that of my colleagues providing teacher education in Birmingham University, is that when teachers do encourage young children to talk about God the results are fascinating and delightful. A rich vein of human experience and spiritual sensitivity can be opened up, and teachers often find that they are not only teaching their children but learning from them.

Many teachers have a concern that such conversations about God might be thought to nurture the faith of young children in God, and thus not only do the work which the churches, mosques, and synagogues should do, but even perhaps indoctrinate children. While this confusion of the role of the religious community and the county school is always possible, and would be a mistake if it occurred, it should not be taken for granted that conversation about God cannot fulfill an educational purpose. The emphasis should not be on teaching

1

children correct or orthodox doctrine about God. This is clearly a matter for the religious communities. Rather the emphasis should be on enriching children's vocabulary and, through conversation, developing images and concepts which will enable children to grapple, at their own level, with the issues and experiences involved in God-talk. To talk about something or someone is not to assume that the thing or person in question exists, but it does affirm the richness and the significance of the idea. The conversational world of many young children is already far too restricted, in spite of and perhaps because of the endless pressure from television and other aspects of the media and the commodity culture. The introduction in school of conversational skills about God should be thought of as offering children a spiritual resource.

Having said this, it is important to emphasize that the conversations reported in this booklet did not take place in school but at home. They often express shared assumptions, values, and beliefs which are normal for the intimacy of family life, but could not necessarily be assumed in school, nor would such an assumption be educationally proper. Allowance should be made for this domestic context when considering the educational appropriateness of these conversational techniques. It would be possible to publish a similar booklet giving examples gathered from the classroom which would be free of this ambiguity. In spite of the fact, however, that the context is domestic rather than professional, one of the purposes of this study is to encourage teachers in exploring the possibilities of God-talk.

A second concern is for the nurture of children in the Christian faith through their families and churches. Not enough has been done to apply contemporary discussions in the social sciences to this area. Many Christian families seem to be stuck fast in the pietistic stereotypes of family life from the past. Others have given up entirely, and leave their children to the tender mercies of the peer group, the media, and the school, hoping perhaps that a viable Christian education will be provided by the local church. Others create a Christian family lifestyle centered around identity with the poor and the marginalized, but do not always enable children to interpret this lifestyle in the light of explicit Christian language and symbol. The art of theological conversation with young children is underdeveloped, and this goes for much of the Christian education in churches as well as homes. God will be real to children brought up in homes and churches where the reality of God through peace and justice issues is made clear, but this requires language about God as well as commitment to peace and justice issues. It is hoped that many Christian parents, and perhaps those from other theistic traditions, will be stimulated by this booklet to think again about the way they introduce prayer and devotion, sacred scripture and commitment to their children.

The intellectual background of this study is provided by three main streams of the social sciences. First, there is the tradition of cognitive stage development associated with Jean Piaget. The often repeated claim that young children are capable of much more than would be expected on Piagetian grounds does not mean that the work of Piaget and his successors has no contribution to make. Piaget emphasized again and again that the socio-genetic unfolding of intelligence, although preserving the same succession of stages, is greatly influenced by the culture, including family and educational background. It may well be that children in modern European cities, for example, are passing through the cognitive stages more rapidly than was the case several decades ago or is now the case in more remote areas. It is also necessary to say that some of those who reject this tradition do not appear to be well informed about its current developments. The work of Ronald Goldman in applying the Piagetian stages to religious thinking in the early 1960s remains of lasting significance, but needs to be supplemented by the work of the American school associated with James Fowler and the Swiss school of Fritz Oser. These offer far more flexible, rich, and imaginative interpretations of the relationship between cognitive stage development and religion than was possible thirty years ago.

The second stream of intellectual tradition is provided by psychoanalysis. There is still a prejudice on the part of many Christian educators and Christian parents against the use of psychoanalysis in understanding religious upbringing. Much of this suspicion springs from the fact that Sigmund Freud himself was so hostile to religion. In the past two decades, however, several aspects of psychoanalytic research have enabled us to see religious development in new ways, and these have an important bearing not only upon the religious lives of adults but upon the lives of children in religious families.

The third intellectual strand is provided by hermeneutics, the art of interpretation. Our understanding of the relationship between readers and books has changed very much in recent years, and these developments in interpretation have an important bearing upon how children are to be taught the Bible, how they are to learn prayers, hear stories and join in conversation. Hermeneutics also influences the way that we ourselves interpret children's conversations, and this is why the discussions which follow each conversation are described as interpretations. They are intended to be creative and suggestive rather than definitive and dogmatic. These conversations are often extremely subtle and could be interpreted in the light of many other frames of reference. What is offered here is, at any rate, an attempt to point one way forward.

Finally, a word must be said about the background of the conversations reported in this book. Parents have unique access into the lives, feelings, and thoughts of their own children. Sometimes the sheer closeness of family living inhibits this access, but in the best situations the parent can study material not easily available to any other adult. What is gained in detail and intimacy is, of course, lost in breadth and wider application.

Almost all the following conversations took place between me and my own children. I have not used individual names of the children because these are not case studies in the development of individual children, but samples of theological conversation offered for interpretation one by one. Some of the conversations were tape-recorded as they took place, but this was rare. In most cases, the conversations were recorded from memory immediately after they took place, but sometimes not until the following day. The actual details of what was said are, naturally, of great importance in this kind of anecdotal study, and I can only say that great care was always taken to be accurate. In spite of this, I have to confess that not all of the entries were carefully dated at the time, and since they took place over a period of several years, I have not always been able to state the precise age of the child in years and months. This is why there are slight variations in the precision with which the ages of the children are mentioned.

I cannot close this introduction without thanking Imogen, Thomas, Elizabeth, and Gabriel for all these and many other conversations, not only about God, but about almost everything else. Your time, Joshua, is yet to come. I would also like to thank my colleagues in the University of Birmingham, whose comments helped me to interpret several of these conversations, especially Michael Grimmett, Julie Grove, and Louise Spencer. Marilyn has mothered not only the children themselves but their language and their conversation. To those who know her this whole study is stamped with her presence.

John M. Hull
Birmingham
4 January 1990

I

THE POWER OF
A CONCRETE THEOLOGY

How can children understand the concept of God when it is so abstract? Should the idea of God be introduced to young children when it is beyond their understanding? When are children ready for talk about God? These are some of the questions which frequently occur to parents and teachers whether at home, in church, or at school.

What Is an Abstract Idea?

The question whether children can understand the idea of God raises a problem about abstract ideas. We must not assume that children, even very young children, cannot understand abstract ideas. After all, what is an abstract idea?

If an abstract idea is an idea about something which you cannot touch or see, then let us consider words like "tomorrow," "darkness," "big," and "heaven." None of these are available to sense perception. "Big," for example, refers to a relationship. The same thing can be big when compared to this but not big when compared to that. You cannot tell whether something is big just by looking at it or touching it. Let us take the familiar children's puzzle about why tomorrow never comes. Children will laugh at the idea that when it comes it is not tomorrow any longer. There is something amusing about a reality which never quite comes within reach. In spite of this, children can use the word "tomorrow" at quite an early age. So in this first sense of "abstract idea," children seem to be able to cope quite well.

Perhaps an abstract idea is simply a generalization. Children can generalize at a very early age. When your child asks, "Is that a dog?" there is surely a general or an abstract idea of dogginess which is being fitted to this particular image or likeness of a dog.

The idea of God is abstract in both of these senses. In the first place, you cannot touch or see God any more than you can touch or see tomorrow. That does not mean that young children cannot talk quite sensibly about God. Secondly, the word "God" is a kind of generalization by which we refer to "the ground and source of everything," "the power of all life," "the ground of being." The word "God" is certainly more difficult than the word "dog." Children see lots of particular dogs and can thus form a general idea of dogginess. They do not see lots and lots of particular gods, unless they are from the Hindu tradition. On the other hand the word "God" is not only an abstract generalization but is also the name of an actual God. He is the God of Abraham and the God and father of our Lord Jesus Christ, the God who brought up Israel out of bondage, who did these particular things. In this sense, God is no more abstract than great grandfather whose exploits are still talked of in the family although he is long since dead, or the baby who will be born six months from now. There are no photographs of the baby and we don't even know if it will be a boy or a girl but it is this particular one.

We see then that since young children can talk quite happily about things which go beyond the senses, and can generalize, there is no reason why they cannot talk quite happily about God. Being abstract does not really seem to be a problem.

Can Children Think Abstractly?

We must distinguish between having an abstract idea and thinking in an abstract way. When the psychologists speak of a child as being a "concrete thinker," they are referring to a certain pattern of thought. The child between the ages of about six and ten years tends to think within the limits of the objects, people, and situations which have been encountered. The older child tends to think in terms of sentences and is no longer confined to the actual situation or object. Abstract thinking is thinking about sentences; concrete thinking is thinking about people and things. This does not mean, however, that children who think in concrete patterns cannot deal with abstract words. A child can enjoy and understand a story about God speaking to the child Samuel just as he or she can appreciate a story about He-man on the Planet Eternia or what grandpa did in the war. The abstract ideas (referring to things which cannot be perceived by the senses) are arranged in concrete ways; that is all. The child will not, of course, understand all there is to understand about God, or He-man, or grandpa, but that does not mean that there will not be a level of understanding and appreciation appropriate to that child.

The expression "back in a minute" is abstract. Understanding it depends upon recognizing the pattern of sound as common to a number of situations so that an expectation is formed. If a baby of 12 months or less is trained in recognizing this pattern of sound and situation, that baby will probably not cry when it is left alone by a parent who says "I'll be back in a minute" provided that the meaning is reinforced by the actual return of the parent very soon. The expression "back in a minute" is abstract in both the senses discussed above: it refers to something intangible and it depends upon the ability to generalize. Nevertheless, the concrete (or in the case of the baby the pre-concrete) thinker can respond to the expression provided it is used with reference to things and people in immediate concrete surroundings.

It is like this with the word God. It will have the meaning of the situations in which it is encountered. God is the one about whom these stories are told, the one to whom prayers are said before going to sleep, the one who is thanked before Sunday lunch, the one who is spoken of in church and at school and in other places. All of this builds up a pattern within which the word God can function adequately. There is the special sense in which the word God is a generalization of many particulars, none of which have ever been seen. We should not, however, be too put off by this difficulty. If the concrete thinking child cannot easily appreciate God as the abstract generalization "ground of being," that without which there would not be anything at all, that which absolutely all things have in common and so on, not much is lost. God can still be appreciated as "the friend of Moses," or as being a Mother or a Father. Moreover, as the child's repertoire of particular, but intangible, uses of the word God grows larger, generalization will be taking place all the time. The generalizations may be locked into particular stories and songs but the first steps will have been taken toward such very general ideas as "being."

Let us summarize what has been said. When the psychologists speak about abstract thinking, they are speaking of abstract patterns of thought. The concrete thinker arranges things in concrete ways, no matter whether the things are available to the senses or are based upon generalizations. There is no reason why the concrete or the pre-concrete thinking child should not think of God in ways which are perfectly adequate for the needs of that child although they will naturally not include all of the ways in which God can be thought of, nor all of the meanings of the word God. Because children cannot understand everything, we must not conclude that they can understand nothing. Children, even when thinking concretely, can think adequately about certain aspects of God, even though some of these aspects are abstract. Concrete thinking styles can cope with aspects both intangible and general.

The Versatility of the Concrete Thinker

Another problem in speaking with children about God is that we frequently underestimate the powers of the concrete thinker. Perhaps it is the word "concrete" which misleads us. We tend to think that the concrete-thinking child will be rigid, unimaginative, lacking in spontaneity and creativity. That is, perhaps, what the word "concrete" suggests to us. Now that we have realized, however, that concrete thinking simply means thinking which deals with the objects and people of immediate experience, we can see that there is no reason why this kind of thinking should not be as varied and as spontaneous as are the things, people, and situations which surround us.

We make things worse by a theological prejudice which exaggerates the degree to which God is beyond time, outside space, and in another world. The God of Christian faith is a concrete God as well as an abstract God, i.e., he is present in our history, in our time and our space, and all things that live are alive with his life. Although the idea of God includes intangible aspects, there are many stories about God in which he is heard, seen, and even touched. These are stories, and therefore still in a way intangible. But we shall not ignore the particular aspects of God by always insisting upon his eternity, omnipresence, and so on.

There are many stories about limitations of the concrete thinker, but you seldom hear stories about the power and flexibility of concrete thinking. The child, for example, asks what God had for supper. The parent replies that God doesn't eat because he has no body. "What?" asks the surprised child. "Do his legs go right up to his neck?" Many people hearing this familiar anecdote conclude that children cannot understand the concept of God. Here is a story which illustrates the expressive power and flexibility of the concrete or indeed the pre-concrete thinker, since the child in question was 3½ years old.

Example 1

CHILD: Was that man's name Mr. Bird?
PARENT: Yes.
CHILD: Was he a bird? (Laughs)
PARENT: Was he like a bird?
CHILD: No.
PARENT: Why not?
CHILD: Birds have feathers. (Laughs)
PARENT: And the man didn't have feathers did he? He had clothes. (Both laugh)
CHILD: And birds have wings.

11

PARENT: Yes.
CHILD: Birds die.
PARENT: So do people.
CHILD: (*Silence*)
PARENT: What does "die" mean?
CHILD: You go to be with God.
PARENT: Where is God?
CHILD: Up in the sky.
PARENT: But up in the sky there are clouds.
CHILD: (*Laughs*) No but I mean when you go up and up and up past the clouds and you go (*speaking in a little high thin voice*) up and up and up and then you come (*whispering*) to a teeny cottage and in that cottage there's God.

Interpretation

This young child knew perfectly well that there was something odd about the literal location of God in a place in the sky, but could not express that oddity in the form of a structure of sentences, arranged so as to reason from one sentence to the next. In other words, the child could not say "when I say 'sky' I am referring to a symbol for that which stands over against this earth and our lives. I am trying to say that God is transcendent, and that the dead are likewise translated somehow into this other plane of reality."

No, the child cannot say that or think in those terms, but the child laughs at the question about clouds. Why? The child knows that in asking the question the parent has playfully and perhaps deliberately misunderstood.The child responds not by moving from concrete to abstract thinking, but by using concrete pictures in literal ways. Moreover, the child dramatizes the situation by speaking in a higher, smaller voice, suggesting that this is something beyond the ordinary plane which is half comical and yet very serious and important, like a shared secret.

The child, being a concrete thinker, cannot respond by drawing attention to the abstract features of the word "up." He can only deal with the problem by pushing the literal meaning of the word further and further. Hence you have to go up and up and up . . . the fact that God's cottage is tiny is the child's concrete way of depicting something which is far away. Cottages seen in the distance do appear tiny. God, as it were, is found in a disappearing point of remoteness. Nevertheless, there is a cottage. The child returns to the homely, the familiar. God is (somehow) an actual person in an actual place but this is not a place like our ordinary places, and his person is not like other people. There are abstract aspects of the word "up" but the child deals with these in a concrete way. He simply repeats the word again and again.

Where Is God?

If the abstract thinker is capable of abstract theological thought, is not the concrete thinker equally capable of concrete theological thought? Concrete theology can be just as faithful and a lot more vivid than abstract theology.

Here is another example. Once again, the subject is "where is God?":

Example 2

FIRST CHILD (aged 3½):	He's in a little cottage in the sky. (*It was the same child as in the previous example*)
SECOND CHILD (aged 6):	No. God is everywhere. God is here (*stabbing finger at tablecloth*) and he's on this crumb (*laughing*).
THIRD CHILD (aged 8):	It means he's in our hearts and in our thoughts and in everything.

Interpretation

The youngest child is thinking in intuitive ways, i.e., pre-concrete. There is a literal acceptance of an image expressed in matter-of-fact spatial language. At the same time, the reality described is special (tone of voice) and far away (in the sky, up and up). The second child is borderline intuitive/concrete. This six-year-old knows that the literal image is not right, or is not considered adequate by some adults, and has heard the expression "God is everywhere," from adults or other children.

The child continues, however, to interpret it in concrete terms. "Everywhere" means here and here and here and there all put together. The child also realizes that this attempt to move into a generalized everywhere by means of multiplying specific places is somehow not quite right, because it leads to a ludicrous result which is both funny and slightly daring: "He's on this crumb." Children in this situation will often continue "Look! I'm squashing God" or "I've eaten him!" (laughing).

The eight-year-old is borderline concrete/abstract. This child knows that "everywhere" in reference to God does not mean a mere cumulation of many specific places but refers to a sort of human universality of emotion and thought, i.e., God is in our hearts and in our thoughts. The child has moved from physical to psychological categories; he has humanized God by speaking of God as dwelling within that which is distinctively and universally human.

You may say "but even the older child could not have been thinking this and could not have said it in those words." Of course, I agree, but my point is that the concrete theology of the third child, although concrete, is flexible and creative and is a genuine theology. What it is saying does not have to be translated into abstract terms to be understood. Its truth lies in itself. This child did not mean that God was in his head the way a pea is in a pod. This would have been simply another example of a specific location. The fact that the child uses the plural and concludes the sentence by referring again to the concept "everywhere" suggests that the child has broken through specific location into some kind of affirmation of a universal but internal relationship. What is said certainly does not lack meaning, and that is true of all three of these children. They are all speaking meaningfully of God at their own levels.

Germs and God

Let us take one final example of children's concrete thinking about the abstract concept of God.

Example 3

FIRST CHILD (aged 6):	Are germs everywhere?
PARENT:	Yes, I supppose germs are just about everywhere. They're certainly everywhere in this house!
FIRST CHILD:	Then germs are like God (*triumphantly*) because God's everywhere. Look (*jabbing at tablecloth*) there's a germ and there's God (*laughs*).
PARENT:	Yes, that's how God is like germs. How is God not like germs?
SECOND CHILD (aged 8):	Germs are many but God is one.

Interpretation

This is another interesting example of the difference between the child who interprets the omnipresence of God in terms of multiplicity of locations and the child who grasps the idea that the omnipresence of God is qualitatively different. Germs, like air and atoms, may be widely, even generally, distributed, but the omnipresence of God is arrived at not through multiplying specific locations but through contrasting location with that which in principle is not located.

The reply of the older child has such a balanced style, such an archaic inversion ("germs are many") that one cannot help wondering whether it has simply been modeled on the formula "God is one" which has been learned, of course, and is not the child's own creation. However, it is difficult to believe that the words were a mere verbalism, uttered from memory without understanding, because the reference to the germs and God was surely a novel feature of this single conversation, and not something the child would have been taught about at school or church. The fact that the child was able to make conversational use of the acquired formula "God is one" and to contrast it with the manyness of the germs seems to me to go beyond the limits of concrete thought.

At the same time, although the younger child cannot spot the difference between germs and God, which requires a judgment of quality, the quantitative similarity is well within this younger child's grasp. Moreover, the younger child spots this similarity for herself. Nobody suggests it to her; the thought just occurs to her. There is thus evidence of a theological concept and a biological concept (both rather abstract ideas) being related in an amusing and creative way. Once again, there is a concrete theology at work here.

Let us summarize. The concrete thinker is often flexible, creative, and versatile. Even the pre-concrete child, the intuitive thinker, can leap from one association to another in a way which often yields adequate and satisfying insights both to child and parent. There is a theological process at work during every pattern of reflection; there is a theology appropriate to the concrete thinker just as there is one available to the abstract thinker. We should not only be challenging children so that their readiness for abstract thinking will be enhanced, but we should be encouraging them to think imaginatively within their immediate experience and in concrete terms.

Concepts, Constructs, and Images

A lot of the problems of parents and teachers in talking with their children about God come from an overemphasis upon concepts. Abstract thinking is sometimes wrongly described as conceptual thinking, whereas as we have seen all thinking expresses and uses concepts in some way or other. What distinguishes abstract from concrete thinking is not that the former makes use of concepts, but that the concepts are related in abstract patterns whereas in concrete thinking the concepts are related in practical, immediate, or experienced contexts. Older children can relate to concepts within the domain of speech alone, which may not be confined to story, while younger children relate most easily to concepts when they are encountered in immediate experience including narration.

By claiming that abstract thinking is conceptual, the impression is given that conceptual thought is the goal of the developmental process, and that pre-abstract thinking is not really thinking at all. This idea is false in several ways. We have already seen that there is conceptual development at every stage of language development, and we need also to realize that conceptual thought is not the only kind of thinking.

There would be some advantages if instead of speaking of concepts we spoke of constructs. A construct is a combination of idea, picture, and attitude toward some aspect of experience, which has developed through experience and will continue to develop. The word construct emphasizes the tentative and the changing nature of thought, and the fact that it is assembled through connecting several bits and pieces of experience. The word concept tends to suggest something more absolute, more finished and coherent, something against which our thinking can be judged rather than something which we are actually thinking. The young child's construct of fatherhood may undergo rearrangement when it is discovered that other children call their male parents "Daddy," and the child's construct "car driver" will develop when it is discovered that there are fathers as well as mothers who drive cars.

One of my own children came back from an outing with the remark "And you know, Daddy, there was a man sitting in mummy's seat," i.e., in the driving seat.

Constructs would be related to each other in concrete ways in middle childhood and in more abstract and theoretical ways in later childhood, just as appears to be the case when we speak of concepts. The pre-concrete child would think intuitively, in the sense that the constructs are less well developed, more impressionistic, liable to rapid swings and changes, and several constructs of a similar reality may exist with little apparent integration. It is that which gives the thought of very young children its delightfully fanciful and creative qualities to the adult ear.

It may also be helpful if we speak of thinking in images. Let us take the thinking which is done in dreams. There is no doubt that dreams do represent a form of thinking, and experiences of insight and even illumination occur to many people when their dreams are interpreted, i.e., translated from dream-thought into conscious thought. The processes of dream-thought are profoundly different from those of conscious thought.

Dream-thought is expressed in images. These may include audible as well as visual images, as when one dreams of hearing someone shouting. It is not that we think in words during waking life and in pictures at night, but that the words and pictures are associated in a different way. With the pressures, dangers, and realities of the external world withdrawn, the sleeping thinker draws upon both recent and remote memories to fashion processes of thought in which emotion is usually dominant. We often sense in our dreams that one thing leads to another with a kind of strange mysterious logic which we find both trivial and sometimes strangely impressive when we consider it from the vantage point of consciousness.

Images are also important in our waking thoughts. This is true in all sorts of trivial ways, e.g., I only recognize you because I have an image of you from yesterday, and our language is studded with metaphors which help us to understand each other. When we speak of a very complicated climatic change affecting the whole of our planet, we speak of the "greenhouse effect," using the homely, concrete image of the greenhouse not only as a convenient shorthand but as a way of enabling us to grasp something of the immense and complex significance of the thing.

The Power of Images

Images are important in our thinking in ways which are far from trivial. There is today a far greater realization of the role of the imagination in scientific thought and discovery than was the case one hundred or even twenty years ago. Scientific thinking is not the cold, rational process of thought it was once imagined to be, but is often experienced as a series of flashing insights, of imaginative leaps, of solutions which just seem to come from nowhere, often driven by stirring new images which relate situations in new and unexpected ways.

Moreover, it is often through our images that we are moved to develop our patterns of thought. Although images always have a specific content, they also seem to have a power to re-pattern our thinking processes. Many adults have found that during times of crisis in their lives, the various phases of re-adjustment have been marked by a certain compelling image which came to the forefront of the mind, and which gradually (or suddenly) gave way to another image that seemed to represent a solution to the problem. The more far-reaching the crisis, the more likely it is that it will be expressed and resolved in images. If a problem is mainly administrative and can be handled in a compartment of life as a contained problem, it can often be sorted out through conceptual thinking, but if the problem is systemic, affecting the whole person, then progress through images seems more common. Perhaps this is why images appear to be most powerful in politics, religion, and in literature.

The reason for this power seems to be the way in which images combine thought, feeling, and experience in a certain vivid, perhaps even concrete way.

Indeed, images are always specific, because they are always representational. Images are not necessarily visual, but they are necessarily structural, i.e., the image is spread out in space or time in the form of a tactile impression, a picture, or an acoustic pattern.

Let us contrast the image of a circle with the concept of a circle. An image of a circle is itself circular. Even if the circle is imagined as seen from the side, in the form of an ellipse, we know through visual experience that if we turn it around it will turn into a circle. The concept of circularity is not, however, circular in form, but is a sentence, a proposition. It is an idea of an infinite line always at the same distance from a certain point. I am speaking here of the concept in its fully developed form, its rational form. The concept has passed through many stages, and when the word "circle" is used by young children to describe various circular images they are doubtless using the construct. Nevertheless, the fully formed concept loses its links with the image logically if not psychologically.

While abstract thinkers continue to have the capacity to think in images and often do, younger children whose constructs are less fully differentiated find it easier to think mainly or even entirely in images. The thinking of the concrete thinker is generally confined to the concept in its image-like form. A young child can learn how to take two apples from four apples and leave two apples behind before the concept of subtraction or the ability to use numbers without objects has been acquired.

There is little doubt that in religious education insufficient attention has been given to the role of images in children's thinking. Overimpressed by the true idea that children's concepts or constructs pass through a gradual process of development, and by the false idea that it is only possible or worthwhile to think about God in purely conceptual ways at the level of abstract patterns, teachers and parents have largely ignored the rich wealth and moving power of religious images. Perhaps this is the secret behind the refusal of Bible stories to go away. This is not just a stubborn conservatism on the part of teachers, but a genuine insight into the continuing power of images.

CHILD: Well, it's small in a way when it goes into something but when it comes out and goes into everything then it's the whole world.
PARENT: Yes. God's body is very big because in a way it is the whole world.
CHILD: (*No comment*)
PARENT: What is God's body then: is it small or is it large?
CHILD: Both.

In the past, but not in recent weeks, this child had been engaged in conversation about the idea that God could be both very old and very young, very large and very small, but (as far as I know) it had not been suggested that God had a body or that his body was small or large. A few days before there had been a discussion about God which had gone like this.

Example 5

CHILD: Does it hurt God when he hits himself with his own hand? Does his head ache when he sneezes?
PARENT: You know the thoughts inside your head?
CHILD: No.
PARENT: Do you have thoughts inside your head that you sometimes don't even speak out?
CHILD: Yes.
PARENT: Well, God is a bit like those thoughts. They are just thoughts; they don't necessarily speak out or have a body.

Interpretation

The sight of the aspirin dissolving in the fizzing water had suggested to this child a way in which God could be both inside your body and yet present in the whole world. The descending scale of size from adult through child to baby suggests the growing concentration of the little bit which nevertheless

spreads through th
gone as far as it can
of the tiny aspirin b
being inside the bod
of the parent's quest
leads the child to re-a
dissolving aspirin to l
the size of the aspirin
child to formulate the
a relationship. The ab
an unseen relationsh
through this series of tl
may be thought of in te
(inside you) and large
divine seeds which, acc
ophers, were both in hur
of nature, the reason ex
experience.

The child was prepai
or prepared to imaginatir
sions which had already g
and relationships. The fac
taneous and creative use c
bility of image-like thinkir
and rational form, and it m
suggesting that this is anyt
the child had been capable
not, perhaps, have had to p
said that, there is somethii
about the way the child puts
interpretation. The images :
penetrate (perhaps) but do n

God's Li

Let us return to the questi
relationships between God and

shown that this
uses spatial ex
between God a
has suggested
there is a prob
terms of imm
abstract ideas
abstractly, wh

Example 6

CHILD (aged
PARENT:

CHILD:
PARENT:

CHILD:
PARENT:

CHILD:

PARENT:
CHILD:

PARENT:
CHILD:
PARENT:

II

THINKING IN
IMAGES

God as a Soluble Aspirin

Example 4

The child (aged 5.2) woke up in the middle of the night with a slight temperature. He watched as the soluble aspirin dissolved in the fizzing water and then drank it. He lay down and got ready for sleep.

CHILD: Why do adults have two aspirins but children only have a half?

PARENT: It's related to the size of your body.

CHILD: How?

PARENT: The bigger your body is, the more you can take. If your body is very big, like the body of an adult, then the two aspirins dissolve and spread around the whole body rather thinly, but if your body is rather small, like that of a child, then it only has to be half an aspirin to spread around that little body.

CHILD: (*After a pause*). And my body is big to Lizzie's (*younger sister*).

PARENT: Yes. And Lizzie's body is big to Gabriel's (*baby*).

CHILD: Yes (*after a pause*) and Gabriel's body is big to (*pause*) . . . to God's.

PARENT: Is God's body very small then?

CHILD: Well, it's small in a way when it goes into some-
          thing but when it comes out and goes into every-
          thing then it's the whole world.
PARENT: Yes. God's body is very big because in a way it is
          the whole world.
CHILD: (*No comment*)
PARENT: What is God's body then: is it small or is it large?
CHILD: Both.

In the past, but not in recent weeks, this child had been
engaged in conversation about the idea that God could be both
very old and very young, very large and very small, but (as far
as I know) it had not been suggested that God had a body or that
his body was small or large. A few days before there had been
a discussion about God which had gone like this.

Example 5

CHILD: Does it hurt God when he hits himself with his
          own hand? Does his head ache when he sneezes?
PARENT: You know the thoughts inside your head?
CHILD: No.
PARENT: Do you have thoughts inside your head that you
          sometimes don't even speak out?
CHILD: Yes.
PARENT: Well, God is a bit like those thoughts. They are
          just thoughts; they don't necessarily speak out or
          have a body.

Interpretation

The sight of the aspirin dissolving in the fizzing water had
suggested to this child a way in which God could be both inside
your body and yet present in the whole world. The descending
scale of size from adult through child to baby suggests the
growing concentration of the little bit which nevertheless

spreads through the whole and when this line of descent has gone as far as it can go the child then seems to connect the idea of the tiny aspirin being inside the body with the idea of God being inside the body. God is now the aspirin. It is the challenge of the parent's question "Is God's body very small then?" which leads the child to re-affirm the cosmic God using the idea of the dissolving aspirin to link the small with the large. The idea that the size of the aspirin is related to the size of the body helps the child to formulate the idea (expressed in images) that bigness is a relationship. The abstract idea of "big," abstract because it is an unseen relationship, a term of comparison, is imaged through this series of thoughts ending up with the idea that God may be thought of in terms of both kinds of relationship, small (inside you) and large (filling everything). One thinks of the divine seeds which, according to the ancient Greek stoic philosophers, were both in human beings and yet were also a principle of nature, the reason expressed everywhere and within human experience.

The child was prepared for the emergence of these images, or prepared to imaginatively construct them, by earlier discussions which had already given a repertoire of images, questions, and relationships. The fact that the child can make such spontaneous and creative use of these materials testifies to the flexibility of image-like thinking. My interpretation is in sequential and rational form, and it must again be emphasized that I am not suggesting that this is anything more than an interpretation. If the child had been capable of putting it in that way, he would not, perhaps, have had to put it in the form of images. Having said that, there is something both stimulating and satisfying about the way the child puts things which is lacking in my adult interpretation. The images satisfy; the abstract interpretations penetrate (perhaps) but do not integrate.

God's Little Cottage

Let us return to the question of how the young child images relationships between God and the world. Earlier examples have shown that this is done in terms of location, and that the child uses spatial exaggeration to suggest the difference in quality between God and human life. At the same time, conversation has suggested to the child that God is also in human life, so there is a problem of dual location. The adult discusses this in terms of immanence and transcendence, which are not only abstract ideas in themselves but ideas which have to be related abstractly, whereas the young child works in images.

Example 6

CHILD (aged 3.10):	Who wins all the battles?
PARENT:	Nobody wins all the battles. You win some, and you lose some.
CHILD:	God wins all the battles.
PARENT:	Well (*hesitation*) perhaps he does in the end, but he loses some along the way.
CHILD:	How does God fight? He's in the sky.
PARENT:	Maybe he fights by helping people. (*Pause*) If God's in the sky why doesn't he fall down?
CHILD:	(*Laughs*) Because he's magic. (*Pause*) And because he lives . . . in a little cottage.
PARENT:	Why doesn't the little cottage fall down?
CHILD:	(*Merry with laughter*) Because it's on the clouds (*pause*) and because God makes it not fall down (*pause, sucks finger noisily*) because God's got his servants who make it not fall down (*pause*) it's on bricks. (*With more confidence and animation*) It's on very big, heavy bricks. They hold it up.
PARENT:	What? On the clouds?
CHILD:	No. There on the earth.
PARENT:	But I thought you said God's cottage was on the clouds.

CHILD:	Well, it goes up in (*emphatically*) the clouds but it stands on earth. Yes (*with growing confidence*), it starts on earth but goes up into the clouds. (*Long pause; turning to parent and in mischievous*) God's in your head.
PARENT:	Is he?
CHILD:	Is that how the reflections come in your glasses? Does God put them there?
PARENT:	(*Only smiles*)

Interpretation

The inadequacy of one image, when pointed out to the child, drives the child into a series of images, each of which is refined or improved as further details occur. A child neatly saves himself from self-contradiction by re-imaging the role of the clouds. The problem is that the child can find no adequate mediation between God and the world. The first mediation is the cottage, then the clouds, then human support, then more substantial support from bricks and so on until at last there is no longer anything mediating, and God's house stands four-square upon the earth.

The child is not unaware of the paradox which this presents, because the question which now lingers in the air but is unexpressed is "where is it?"

At this point, the philosophical child changes direction from transcendence to immanence. Now God is no longer located above the earth but in the human. This may also be the result of the trend of the thought from the sky down to the earth and so into human beings. God is again imaged as being within, and as causing physical phenomena associated with the head such as reflections in one's glasses. The question "How does God get in and out of people's heads?" would doubtless occur to the child, at some time.

It is important to emphasize that this conversation is conducted in the spirit of teasing. The child is both amused and provoked; it becomes a little contest. The child is delighted with his victories, puzzled by their temporary nature. The final exchange about the head is delivered in a teasing manner but with triumph, as if the child is saying "Of course, there's another way of thinking about this whole thing, isn't there? But that would start us on a lot of new stuff!"

The idea of God's house standing on the earth and stretching up into the clouds reminds us of the Tower of Babel while the speculation about how the divine presence is mediated reminds us of many religious myths. Mythic thinking works very well for this child and enables him to explore a variety of ways of conceiving God.

My Heart Told Me

Example 7

CHILD (aged 5¾):   I've got four invisible friends.
PARENT: Who are they?
CHILD: Well, there's Mary, Jesus, God and the Holy Spirit.
PARENT: (*Laughing*) Who told you that?
CHILD: My heart told me that (*pause*) my brain told me that (*laughs*) Does my brain talk to me? Does it say hello (child's name)?

Interpretation

This child is attending a Catholic infant school. It is possible that the image of the "invisible friend" was remembered from something said at the school, and the fact that the three Persons of the Trinity are referred to correctly together with Mary supports this suggestion. It is also possible that the "heart" as the locus of religious devotion has come from the school. Be that as it may, this is a useful image for the child, and it is noteworthy that it was repeated spontaneously and happily at home.

Perhaps more interesting is the way in which the image and the question "Who told you that?" seems to stimulate the child into an awareness of image-making processes. Is it the heart or the brain? Are there two? Where do thoughts and images come from? Are we in charge of our own thoughts? The idea of God as resident within human thoughts, ideas, and speech does not lessen the transcendent power of these ideas, but enables the child to begin a process of constructive criticism. If attention is never drawn to speech itself and to imagery in particular as the context of God, if attention is always upon God and never upon God-talk, there is a danger that God becomes too much a part of the external world and insufficiently a bridge for the child's inner and outer experiences.

A Very Big Idea

It is better for children to have too many images than too few. Indeed, I am not sure that a child can have too many images of God. It is certainly far more common for a child to be starved of images or even fixated on one image into which every other aspect of God must fit.

Sometimes it is right to contradict an image; usually, however, the child's images should be confirmed and extended. It is best to follow the lead of a child and to encourage the child as theological image-maker.

Example 8

FIRST CHILD (aged 5.2):	Is God the air?
PARENT:	No. God's not the air but he's a bit like the air.
SECOND CHILD (aged 3.9):	Is God the ceiling?
PARENT:	No, God is not the ceiling, but he is a bit like the ceiling.
FIRST CHILD:	Is he a round baby?

PARENT:	No, he's not a round baby, but he's a bit like a little baby because he's new and fresh.
SECOND CHILD:	Is he invisible?
PARENT:	Yes he is.
FIRST CHILD:	Is he like a round baby with wings flying through the air? *(general laughter).*
PARENT:	God is a bit like lots of things but he's not exactly like anything.
SECOND CHILD:	Why not?
PARENT:	Because God is unique. God hasn't really got a shape at all.
FIRST CHILD:	Why hasn't he got a shape?
PARENT:	Because God is a sort of idea. Have ideas got shapes?
FIRST CHILD:	*(Pause, then laughs)* No.
PARENT:	Well, God is a bit like a very big idea.

Interpretation

The 18 months difference between these two children is evident. The older child identifies God with the air, the younger child with the ceiling. The ceiling is visible, and the younger child goes on to the quality of invisibility later in the discussion.

The parent's intention is to move from ideas of identity to ideas of likeness. In this way the conversation moves from the nature or essence of God to images or models of God. If children can be helped to use the expression "like" when speaking of God, the way is open for many comparisons. The parent agreed that God was a bit like a ceiling partly in order to avoid discouraging the younger child, and partly because God might indeed be thought of as being above us, higher than us, arching over us in protection and so on. There is, of course, a whimsical aspect of the younger child's observations. The child will ask about the first thing its eyes happen to rest on, and in this case the ceiling was possibly suggested by the comment about the air.

With the image of the round baby, the next step is taken; the parent begins to suggest aspects of the image which may be like God. Even if an entire image is not applicable, aspects of it may be. With the thought of invisibility, the discussion moves from images to qualities. Of course, it would once again have been possible to have said that in some senses God is invisible and yet he is also visible in all beautiful things and so on. The younger child, however, needs more affirmation. She needs to know that she is on the right track, whereas the older child has a richer fund of images to draw upon and can make more distinctions. No doubt the image of the winged cherub has been seen in religious art, whether in books or on Christmas cards.

The pause that follows laughter is often a good moment to introduce a new idea or to sum things up. Hence the change in the discussion at this point. It doesn't matter if the children don't know the word "unique." This may be their first introduction to the word, but its meaning is clear enough in context and they will return to it later. The discussion concludes with the parent suggesting a new image, that of an idea. Like the other images, there are only certain aspects of this which apply, hence the concluding thought that God is a bit like this, but only a bit.

How Many Gods in All the Worlds?

The imagination of children should be fertilized with images drawn from many story-cycles in which human emotions and exploits, a range of human and divine characters, and the many-sided relationships between the divine and human worlds are illustrated. It is a mistake to confine the imagination of the child entirely to the Bible and to the Christian tradition. My own experience is that the stimulus of ideas and images from other traditions always quickens the child's curiosity and leads to greater enjoyment and greater use in daily life of religious symbols. In the examples that follow, the children had been reading the myths and legends of the Norse gods and heroes.

Example 9

CHILD (aged 5.4):	When do the questions come about Thor?
PARENT:	What do you mean by that?
CHILD:	About Thor and the Giants.
PARENT:	Do you want some questions about Thor and the giants?
CHILD:	Yes.
PARENT:	What is Thor?
CHILD:	He's (*pause*) a god (*emphatically*).
PARENT:	What's a god?
CHILD:	A god is an invisible person because he's up in the sky (*emphatically*).
PARENT:	And what is Thor's hammer?
CHILD:	A thunderbolt.
PARENT:	Is that what Thor's hammer stands for?
CHILD:	Yes.
PARENT:	Is it a real hammer?
CHILD:	(*Pause*) Er, er (*pause*) I don't think so.
PARENT:	What is it really then?
CHILD:	I don't know.
PARENT:	Makes a big loud noise though, doesn't it?
CHILD:	Yes (*pause, then shouting dramatically*) a thunderbolt really.
PARENT:	That's right.
CHILD:	Not really a hammer.
PARENT:	Not really a hammer?
CHILD:	No. A thunna-derra bolta (*with mock emphasis*).
PARENT:	What is Thor really then?

CHILD:	A god and not Thor. (*repeats the Thor in a whisper: a god and not Thor*).
PARENT:	A god and not Thor?
CHILD:	Yes, 'cos (*pause*) 'cos he's a god but his name is not Thor.
PARENT:	Why not?
CHILD:	Well it says that.
PARENT:	It says his name is Thor.
CHILD:	Yes (*pause*) what's the point?
PARENT:	I'm not sure. How many gods are there?
CHILD:	I don't know.
PARENT:	Lots?
CHILD:	Lots, hundreds . . .
PARENT:	Or just one?
CHILD:	Four, I think.
PARENT:	Four?
CHILD:	Odin, Loki, Thor, and Freier.
PARENT:	Yes. They're the Nordic gods, aren't they?
CHILD:	Yes.
PARENT:	Can you think of any Greek gods?
CHILD:	Have we got a Greek god?
PARENT:	Not exactly.
CHILD:	Is ours an English god?
PARENT:	(*Laughs*) Yes, I suppose he is.
CHILD:	How many gods in all the worlds?
PARENT:	I don't know. Thousands, I suppose.
CHILD:	Thousands, hundreds, millions, trillions, billions.
PARENT:	Some people say there's only—
CHILD:	Two, three (laughs).
PARENT:	Some people say there's only one.
CHILD:	What's three and a hundred?
PARENT:	One hundred and three.

Interpretation

God has many names, yet his names are one. Numbers, as well as names are symbols. Huge numbers can symbolize the immensity and infinite variety of the divine, while small numbers can emphasize the simplicity and unity of the divine.

The names and numbers of God vary throughout the Bible. In the Psalms, for example, God is often shown in conversation with other gods, and at certain points God reveals a new name. He has new mysterious names that nobody yet knows, and he is known in many different ways.

Does He Go One, Two, Three, Four, Five?

Sometimes the mythology of the ancient world (Greece, Rome, Egypt) has an important contribution to make. Not only are religious ideas and symbols powerfully and beautifully represented, but the narrative form is vivid for both child and adult, and the many similarities to the religious imagery of the Christian tradition offers opportunities for conversation.

Sometimes numbers and the relationships which they express help a child to catch a glimpse of God in a way different from the very concrete picture of Thor with his hammer or the little round baby with wings.

Example 10

CHILD (aged 5.8):	How old will I be when Gabriel is one?
PARENT:	You'll be six.
CHILD:	How old will Gabriel be when I am 21?
PARENT:	16.
CHILD:	When I am 99?
PARENT:	94.
CHILD:	How old will he be when I am 144?
PARENT:	Nobody lives that long.
CHILD:	Except God.
PARENT:	Yes, of course. Well God lives forever.
CHILD:	Does he get to be 100 and then start all over again? Does he go one, two, three,

four, five till 100 and then become a
baby and go one, two, three, four, five
until there's another 100 and so on?

PARENT: Not exactly. You'see, God has all the ages
in him. He is one and he is five and he is
20 and he is 1,000. He's got all those
ages in him already. But we've only got
the ages we've already lived through, like
you've got one, two, three, four, and five.

CHILD: Yes, we don't need to have all the ages in
us, 'cos we've got God in us, haven't we?

PARENT: Well (*laughing*) that's one way of putting
it!

CHILD: (*Laughing and throwing arms round parent*)
Daddy, daddy, daddy (*squeezing tightly*)
that's one way of putting it is it? That's
one way of putting it, is it? (*laughs
uproariously*)

Interpretation

The discussion shows the interest young children take in
the human life cycle. Young children are interested in babies,
because a baby is the immediate past of the child, past but
already forgotten. The social reinforcement provided by birth-
days, and the age stratification of school classes leads to an
intense awareness of the numbers 4, 5, 6, and so on. Young
children are often intrigued to discover that the relationship
between age and increased size does not continue, and that
adults of various sizes may be the same age while adults of the
same age may be of various sizes.

Numerical sequence offers some understanding not only of
adult life but of assurance against the threat of death, since the
child is told that people always die and that usually people are
old (have lots of numbers) when they die. Death is when the

numbers stop. Birth is when the numbers start, presumably. Here is another case.

Example 11

CHILD (aged 4):   First you're two then you're three then you're four then you're eight then you're 23 . . . what is it then?

PARENT: Then you're 30 and then you're 35 and then you're 40 and so on.

CHILD: And then there's 65 and 83 and a million . . . when do the numbers stop?

PARENT: The numbers don't stop. They go on for ever and ever and ever.

CHILD: Wow!

Interpretation

It is impossible to tell in this context whether the parent had misunderstood the child or not. Was the question about human mortality or about numerical sequence? In any case, number, chronology, and the life cycle are related in the child's experience and are certainly a way of interpreting death.

Against the finite human life cycle, God as including all stages of the life cycle and as himself beyond all cycles stands out in contrast. Although the young child's grasp of this may be fleeting and intuitive, it may also at times be vivid and insightful. It may provide an effective alternative image to the one which fixes upon God as being solely in human form, especially in the shape of an old man. If God is an old man, why does he not die? The point is that God has all the numbers in him, and is thus always young and always old.

Can Jesus Stick to Water?

Amongst the various names of God, the name of Jesus will often be mentioned, and the problem of the relationship between Jesus and the Father God will often make an early appearance.

Example 12

FIRST CHILD (aged 4.1):	Jesus flies through the air and can do anything.
SECOND CHILD (aged 5.7):	No he doesn't. That's God! *(laughs)* Jesus was born a man on earth like us. It's God who can fly through the air and do everything.
FIRST CHILD:	No, it's Jesus isn't it daddy?
SECOND CHILD:	No, it's God. Jesus was a man like we are. God can do anything and can fly through the air, can't he daddy?
PARENT:	Jesus was a wonderful man who showed us a lot about what God is like, and it is God who is everywhere and who knows about everything.

Example 13

CHILD (aged 3.9):	Can I have one of those stories about Jesus?
PARENT:	Would you like one about how he ran away from home?
CHILD:	*(astonished)* How could he? He can't fly can he? *(laughs)*
PARENT:	This is not a story about when Jesus was in heaven with God. It's a story about how, when he was born as a little baby and lived in a house like we do, he ran away from his house one day.
CHILD:	Oh.

Example 14

CHILD (aged 5.7):	(While brushing teeth) Can Jesus stick to water? Can Jesus make water stick to him?
PARENT:	No, Jesus can't make water stick to him.
CHILD:	Why can't he? Can God make water stick to him?
PARENT:	No. God's not like that. Jesus and water are different kinds of things, and God and water are different kinds of things.
CHILD:	Why?
PARENT:	Well, where on God would the water stick? Would it stick to his hands? Would it stick to his hair?
CHILD:	(*Laughs*) No, because God hasn't got a body.
PARENT:	Maybe he would dry himself off with a cloud.
CHILD:	(*Laughs*)
PARENT:	Can water stick to air?
CHILD:	No. Can God do all the things we can't do?
PARENT:	No, there's lots of things we can't do and God can't do either.
CHILD:	What?
PARENT:	Well, God can't make time go backwards.
CHILD:	(*Riding on parent's shoulders and turning on light in bedroom*) No, and God can't turn on the light without a switch.
PARENT:	Yes, maybe. And God can't make two and two six, can he? because they're four.
CHILD:	Yes. Can God make you fly without wings? (*Conversation turned to mathematical questions*).

Thinking in Images

Interpretation

The theme of flying is important partly because it is a way of linking heaven and earth, and partly because it is an impressive example of power. Jesus as the one who is both in heaven and on earth is an obvious candidate for flying, and as the one who shares in the power of God, he can do anything. These ideas are reinforced, perhaps, by stories about the miracles of Jesus, and the Ascension where Jesus rises through the clouds.

Much of the confusion between God and Jesus can be avoided by emphasizing that Jesus was a baby, then a child, and then an adult who lived a human life like ours and there are stories about what he did. For Christian children, God is best approached through Jesus when the humanity of Jesus is emphasized. Otherwise, instead of mediating between humanity and God, Jesus will simply share in the magical qualities of God. As far as the latter are concerned children can be helped to understand that there are limits to the things you can say if you want to talk sense, and silly things don't become sensible just because you put the name of God in the sentence. That only makes God a silly word, and does not make the silly sentence sensible.

Nothing and Nowhere

In these examples we have been considering names and numbers. The expression "nothing" also has a place in the thinking of children about God. Nothing is the beginning of the numbers, the place before the numbers start, and what you have got left when all the numbers have gone.

Example 15

CHILD (aged 5.8):   (*Walking home from school on a bright, sunny afternoon*) Does everything have a shadow?

PARENT:	Yes, as long as the sun is shining. Where do your shadows go when the sun isn't shining?
CHILD:	Nowhere.
PARENT:	Where is nowhere?
CHILD:	Nowhere's nowhere. (*Pause*) Nowhere is where God is.
PARENT:	Nowhere is where God is?
CHILD:	Well, you see God's up in a cloud and you can't see him through the cloud because he's all surrounded by the cloud but you see him when you die. God is the only thing you can see when you're dead.

Example 16

CHILD (aged 5.9):	Is anything bigger than God?
PARENT:	(*drawing a figure eight in sand with a little figure ten inside one of the loops*) Which is bigger, the eight or the ten?
CHILD:	Eight.
PARENT:	So you'd rather have eight sweeties than ten, would you?
CHILD:	No.
PARENT:	So which is bigger?
CHILD:	Eight is bigger but the ten is better.
PARENT:	You can write the eight any size you like, but ten will always be more valuable.
CHILD:	Yes.
PARENT:	God is always better. He is the most valuable thing there is.

Interpretation

It has been shown how significant in the thinking of the young child are names and numbers, and how these lend

38

themselves to discussions about qualities, powers, identities, contrasts of size and value, and ideas about repetition, cycles, beginnings and endings. Such language enables children to speak of God without using human parallels, so that without denying the value of human beings as pictures of God, it is realized that God-talk need not be confined to this.

III

THE MORAL ORDER,
PRAYER, AND THE BIBLE

He'd Jump into Himself

The super-heroes of comic and cartoon often provide the first fertile source of imagery for the young child who is exploring the images of God.

Example 17

PARENT:	(*Following a discussion about the exploits of Superman*) Who can jump higher then, God or Superman?
FIRST CHILD (aged 5 years):	God.
SECOND CHILD (aged 6½):	Yes, God can jump better.
PARENT:	But can God jump? What would happen if he jumped?
SECOND CHILD:	(*with a flash of excitement*) He'd jump into himself. He's already there. He's everywhere. He doesn't need to jump.
PARENT:	(*laughing*) So who can go faster, God or Superman?
SECOND CHILD:	It takes Superman a millionth of a second to go round the world.
PARENT:	And what about God?

SECOND CHILD:	He's there already.
PARENT:	So however fast Superman travels, God is always there first because he's there already.
SECOND CHILD:	Yes. (*laughs with delight*)

Interpretation

I have asked many adult groups these questions, and almost always adults' first response is that God can jump higher and run faster than Superman. Many of the divine attributes, however, are not relative but absolute. When we say that God is omniscient, we are not claiming that he knows a bit more or a lot more than the winner of the "Brain of Britain" contest. The question "Who knows more, Brain of Britain or God?" is misleading since the knowledge of God is in principle complete. The same is true of the divine presence. God cannot be said to move however rapidly from one point to another in the universe, since his presence and his knowledge are co-extensive. There is no place where he is not. God is not mobile, because he is not finite. There is therefore no comparison between the speed of Superman and the speed of God. Superman and God are different categories of being, different orders of existence. No matter how fast Superman were to travel, he would continue to be a mobile point, in time and space. Increasing speed does not turn into omnipresence any more than increasing knowledge turns into omniscience.

The younger of the two children remained mystified by this conversation, but the older child had grasped the point through a kind of cartoon image of God jumping only to find another image of God already there, a bit like cartoons where somebody bounces forward on a pogo stick so rapidly that a little image of himself is left behind at each bounce, only in reverse, so that the image of God is there already. There is no point in bouncing because you are already there. The concrete image enables the child to make these distinctions.

Does God Love Burglars?

The power of the super-hero enables the child to imagine the greatest power possible.

Example 18

CHILD (4 years): Who would win the fight, God or He-man?
PARENT: God.
CHILD: What if Teela helped He-man?
PARENT: God would still win.
CHILD: What if it were He-man, and Teela, and Stratos?
PARENT: God is greater.

Interpretation

It is such epics as He-man which lead a child into the world of baddies and goodies. A "baddy" is against "Us," while a "goody" is on our side. The division is simply between those who threaten us and those who support us. The distinction is not a moral one, and there are no ambiguities.

Example 19

PARENT: (*telling Bible story*) Well, Saul tried to be a good king but he didn't always succeed.
FIRST CHILD (aged 3.11): (*with astonishment*) Wasn't he a goody?
SECOND CHILD (aged 7.5): (*with a knowledgeable air*) People are only goodies and baddies on the TV and in comics. In real life goodies and baddies are mixed up.

43

FIRST CHILD: Everybody's a goody and
                baddy. Mummy said so.
                (*triumphantly*) Why have they
                got swords then?

Interpretation

The older child has acquired a formula and can repeat it with some degree of understanding. The younger child is determined not to be beaten by his older sister, and seizes upon the sword as the obviously aggressive weapon. If they are not entirely and thoroughly bad, why are they fighting against us?

There comes a time, however, when God will be thought of as being opposed to baddies not merely in the sense that he is stronger and is on "our side" but in the moral sense. God is opposed to baddies not just because they are opposed to him, but because he is good.

Example 20

CHILD (aged 5.6):   Does God love burglars?
PARENT: God loves the burglars, but he doesn't
                    like what they do.
CHILD: Is that because they are baddies?
PARENT: Yes, God loves them but he doesn't like
                    what they do.
CHILD: Is this because the things they do are bad?
PARENT: Yes.

Interpretation

God is here contrasted with badness. In the earlier thinking of this child, God was merely stronger than badness and opposed to it. Now God is seen as different from badness not merely by being stronger but by being of a different quality. This child was passing through a period when he was interested in the relative degrees of love, and parents were often asked if they loved one or the other of their children more than the others, or whether the parents loved God more than they loved the children and so on. The young child's exploration of ideas such as goodness, badness, power and love is always in the context of the actual relationships of morality and love within which the child is living.

Watching from a Cloud

Questions about the goodness of God often relate to his power and his apparent inactivity. Superman intervenes; God does not. The young child is sometimes capable of appreciating the shock of Auschwitz and of Calvary: the God who does nothing.

Example 21

On the morning news there was an item about a siege of a Palace of Justice in a South American city. The building had been occupied by guerilla fighters and some of the judges had been shot. In the end, government troops stormed the building with extensive loss of life.

PARENT: Do you know what a judge is?

CHILD (aged 5.3): Yes. Why did they shoot them? Was it because the guerillas were friends with the prisoners?

PARENT: (*described the events*) . . . and so you see, everyone just started shooting at each other. They didn't stop to talk; they just began firing.

CHILD: They just battled straight away, didn't they? (*Pause*) Where was God?

PARENT: Well, that's a very good question.
CHILD: Was he watching from a cloud?
PARENT: Well, in a way, but it was a situation of
                    evil, wasn't it? Violent men on both sides
                    were fighting and killing each other.
CHILD: (*Passionately*) He was nowhere! (*Hitting the
                    table*) Nowhere! Nowhere!
PARENT: (*Nonplussed*)

Interpretation

The situation presented an impasse to the thought of both parent and child. The transcendent solution, in which God is the all-knowing spectator sitting on a cloud, fails because of the enormity of the suggestion that anyone, especially someone with God's power, could just watch. The solution which sees God in the midst of life, God already in the situation, also fails because of the difficulty in discovering any traces of a divine presence. Violent men were just battling it out. God was nowhere. Although physically and metaphysically, God is everywhere, are there situations of such evil that God can be absent? Is there a "Godless" situation and even a "Godless" world?

Praying to God for a Six

Prayer is often introduced to the young child as if it made possible a divine intervention, or even as if without prayer a divine intervention would be less likely or impossible. Prayer is thus linked to God's power, and the way is opened up for many disappointments and disillusionments in the child's experience of God. The unreliability of prayer as a means of gaining divine intervention quickly leads to ritual, defensive qualifications, and to the idea of prayer and of God as lucky charms.

Example 22

The children were playing Ludo having just returned from church.

FIRST CHILD (aged 5.6): I'm going to pray to God for a six (*a six is thrown*). There! it was because I prayed to God. Why don't you pray to God?

SECOND CHILD (aged 4): Dear God bless this food amen. (*A two is thrown*)

FIRST CHILD: Never mind. You can try again when it's your turn.

Example 23

Mother had just praised the younger child for eating up her dinner.

FIRST CHILD (aged 5.6): You never praised me! (*throws himself into mother's arms sobbing*).

SECOND CHILD (aged 4): (*Loudly*) Why don't you pray to God then?

FIRST CHILD: (*Crying even more loudly*) But I do!

Example 24

(*Child in bed about to go to sleep*)

PARENT: Would you like to say the Lord's prayer?

CHILD (aged 4): No.

PARENT: What about "Teach us good Lord"?

CHILD: No.

PARENT:	Would you like to learn a little, new prayer?
CHILD:	Yes.
PARENT followed by CHILD:	In the name . . . of the Father . . . and the Son . . . and the Holy Spirit. Amen.
CHILD:	Would you like me to teach you a prayer?
PARENT:	Yes.
CHILD followed by PARENT:	Dear God . . . thank you . . . for this . . . dinner. Amen. They were the same size weren't they?
PARENT:	Yes. Just the same.
CHILD:	Why can't you see them?
PARENT:	If the prayers were written down we could see them but if we only speak them, then we can't see them.
CHILD:	God can see them because all the things that the people can't see God can see.
PARENT:	Yes.

Example 25

Both children were helping to look for mummy's glasses. The younger child suddenly found them.

FIRST CHILD (aged 4.2):	I've found them! I've found them!
PARENT:	(*from downstairs*) Oh, you are a good girl. Bring them down to me.
SECOND CHILD (aged 5.8):	I was helping too because I was praying to God. I was praying to God that you would find them sooner or later.

48

Example 26

The child woke up about 11 p.m. crying. Father went upstairs to comfort her.

CHILD (aged 4.6): I want mummy to come up and talk to me
too.
PARENT: Mummy is sewing. She'll come up later.
CHILD: Grandma was sewing. She was sewing a
new jumper for me for next year.
PARENT: That was kind of grandma. Aren't you
lucky to have two grandmas and two
grandpas?
CHILD: Yes. I've got everything I need.
PARENT: Yes, you have.
CHILD: I've got plenty of toys and . . . games to
play with.
PARENT: Yes, and you've got a nice warm bed to
sleep in, and clothes to keep you warm.
CHILD: Is God really everywhere like (older
brother) says he is?
PARENT: Yes, he is everywhere.
CHILD: Is he even on my head?
PARENT: Yes. He's everywhere, but especially when
we are talking about him.
CHILD: Like when we are praying.
PARENT: Yes. But also when we are just talking.
CHILD: Like we're talking about him now.
PARENT: Yes, and in all our talking. It's nice to talk
isn't it?
CHILD: Yes.
PARENT: You go to sleep now then.

Prayer presents rich possibilities for developing images of
God. Questions about God's way of life, his daily routine, and so
on are often evoked by the context in which he is about to be

addressed. The following example is a young child's first spontaneous theological observation, and it took place in the context
of preparing to go to sleep, although there had been no particular invitation to pray.

Example 27

CHILD (aged 2.6): Does God go to bed when he's sleepy?
PARENT: God never gets sleepy. He always stays
wide awake.
CHILD: Doesn't he have a bed then?
PARENT: Well, he always stays wide awake, to look
after things and to love us.
CHILD: Oh (goes to sleep).

Interpretation

This child had been taken by a neighbor to a school mass
only a few days earlier where he had, for the first time, spontaneously joined in the prayer time. His prayer, which he made
up, was simply "Help, God."

Prayer Conversations

Prayer is based upon images of speaking and listening. In
prayer, human relationships with God are constructed on the
basis of the human experience of conversation. As with all
images of God, this should be placed beside other images.
Proliferation of images enriches the child's conversational
repertoire and helps to prevent rigidity in thinking about God.
Metaphors based on God as seeing and listening should be
placed alongside language which refers to God as knowing or as
being. The tendency of prayer to suggest that God is like a
person doing things also needs to be supplemented (not

corrected) by images of God as the sustainer rather than the intervener. Both these points are illustrated in the following examples.

Example 28

The older child (aged 5.7) woke up around midnight and wanted prayers to be said. He then sang "Away in a Manger" while the parent joined in the last verse "Take us to heaven to be with thee there."

FIRST CHILD:	(*laughing*) To be with God?
SECOND CHILD (aged 4.1):	(*Had been joining in the singing*) Do we go to be with God?
PARENT:	Yes, but we are always with God.
SECOND CHILD:	Yes, but we can't see God, can we?
PARENT:	(*No reply*)
SECOND CHILD:	But can he see us?
PARENT:	Well, he knows about us.
SECOND CHILD:	Oh.

Example 29

CHILD (aged 5.5):	(*watching snow falling*) Is God sending the snow down? Is he making the snow come down?
PARENT:	Well, he's not actually up there sending it down. It snows because of certain conditions in the clouds.
CHILD:	Well, does God make the conditions? (*Repeats with emphasis*): Does he make the conditions then?
PARENT:	The conditions are natural, and God is the giver of everything that is natural and beautiful.

I cannot leave this section about prayer without giving two examples of the graces before meals offered by young children. In both cases (which were separate in time) the family grace had been said together, and the child had then volunteered its own additional grace.

Example 30

CHILD (aged about 3):   Dear God, thank you for this food. Make us eat it as you would eat it.

Example 31

CHILD (aged 3.11):   Dear God, thank you for this food, and if there is anything we don't like, we will give it to you, and you will eat it all up. Amen.

In these two graces we see God as the collaborator with the child in conflicts with parents over food. How convenient it would be to avoid the parental wrath by having a God near at hand to dispose of everything which the child does not want! God is the alibi, who will make us like things, make us do things, and if we do not, then he must be to blame. In both cases, the conventional expression of gratitude is followed by the child's real thoughts about what God is contributing to the situation.

If You Had Made the Promise

Many of the conversations with young children which we have been discussing arose spontaneously during family meals or during the quiet times at the end of the day. Often these conversations have centered around the divine attributes, the character of God, and the peculiarities of his or her being. Little has been said so far about the story as a way of sharing God-talk with young children, and it is to this that we now turn.

In prayer God is directly addressed. In conversation about the idea of God, the focus of interest is on the word "God" itself, the limits of its meaning and its relation with other words. In the story, God appears as an actor in a drama. We catch a moment in the life and history of God. This makes it possible to raise questions about the relationships between God and human beings, and to ask about God's motives and interests. Moreover, the story provides a screen upon which the drama of the child's own life can be projected. Relationships with parents, other children, and with the past and future of the child's own life can all be considered in the light of the story, and related to the story of God.

Example 32

Jephthah promised God that if he was victorious in battle he would sacrifice to God the first living creature which greeted him when he came home. To his dismay he was greeted by his only daughter. Nevertheless, he kept his promise to God. After the parent had read this story to his daughter the following conversation took place.

CHILD (about 5 years):	What would you have done?
PARENT:	What do you mean, what would I have done?
CHILD:	If you had made that promise.
PARENT:	I wouldn't have been so silly as to make such a silly promise in the first place.
CHILD:	But if you had? What would you do then, if you had made the promise?
PARENT:	If I had made such a silly promise, I would be even sillier to keep it, wouldn't I?

CHILD: Yes. (*Pause*) Goodnight, daddy. (*Calls
                              out after parent has left room*) I love
                              you daddy.

Interpretation

The father has become Jephthah and the child has become
Jephthah's daughter. The question has become one of safety
and of trust, and of the place which the child holds in the affec-
tions and commitments of the parent. It is noteworthy that in the
story Jephthah takes the initiative in offering this promise to
God. There is no indication that God entered into the agreement, or that it occurred to Jephthah to ask God what he
thought about such a promise. Be that as it may, the parent
confronted with such persistent questioning in such an earnest
manner must declare without ambiguity where his commitment
lies. If he does not love his daughter whom he has seen, how can
he love God whom he has not seen? The defense of the child's
sense of safety requires an attack upon the fanaticism of
Jephthah, and this may well be the young child's first introduction into the way in which religion can distort and blight
human life. Within the context of a trusted relationship with an
adult, the young child can accept this and emerge from it
stronger. The farewell words of the child bear witness to this.

In the case of older young people, the question becomes
one of identity and of autonomy. What bargains and contracts
have been entered into behind my back? What have my parents
committed me to of which I know nothing? Who am I, that other
people, even God, can decide my fate? In the following example
a 15-year-old girl had been studying the story of Jephthah as
part of her religious education at school. She burst into the
living room where her mother was watching the television.

Example 33

DAUGHTER: You know, mummy, I'm studying Jephthah in
            the Old Testament.

MOTHER: Really dear, what do you think of him?
DAUGHTER: (*passionately*) He was a bastard!
MOTHER: Oh. Why was that?
DAUGHTER: He didn't care what happened to her. He only
             thought of himself. He had to keep his prom-
             ises whatever happened. It didn't matter about
             her.
MOTHER: Oh. I see. Well . . .
DAUGHTER: (*kneeling beside mother and bursting into tears*)
             And you know mummy we don't even know
             her name.

Interpretation

There was an age span of ten years between these two girls. The issues which reverberate for the younger child are not those which are of significance for the older one. The teenager protests against the helplessness and the anonymity of the young caught in the military and political maneuvers of the older generation. For the little girl dependency is acceptable provided that it is in a context of safety. For every phase of life there will be a horizon of meaning which will meet with Jephthah and his daughter.

IV

FAMILY LIFE AND
THE ORIGINS OF GOD-TALK

We have been exploring examples of conversations about religion between children and parents. Perhaps we can try to formulate some general observations. I am mainly thinking of the home, but perhaps some of these remarks will have application to children in school.

God and Intermediate Space

"Intermediate space" is used to describe that area of a child's consciousness which is neither entirely subjective nor objective. Thoughts are inside your head but the sound of the telephone ringing is outside. The distinction between inside and outside is not innate but is learned. At first, there is neither inside nor outside but simply an undifferentiated world of sensation. The skin is important as the membrane which divides inside from outside, but there is traffic between the two. The ways in which this traffic is managed is a vital aspect of the development of personality in childhood.

First we may think of the mouth, and its function in receiving nourishment, which comes from the outside and goes inside. Next, we may consider the products of the bladder and the bowels, which come from the inside and are expelled. Finally, we may think of the genitals, of the power of the vagina to include and of the penis to penetrate.

Not only does the skin thus open and close to admit and expel the world outside, but so do the eyes and, in their different ways, the other senses. The mouth opens in speech which has an effect upon the outside world. Mother comes when I cry. Images are perceptions which have remained inside and become memories. They have a bridging function, and link the world of inner experience with the world of outer stimulus.

This area of intermediate space can also be called "transitional" because it is the area where the inner and the outer merge. This intermediate or transitional space is occupied by objects, some of which are internal images like the memory of the face of mother, and others are objects in the outside world which have been charged with emotional significance. The corner of the blanket which the young child sucks when lonely or sad might be an example of such a transitional object. It represents the mother's breast and is meaningful to the child because of these associations. From the corner of the blanket many children will go on to the teddy bear's ear, and a whole variety of dolls and other toys, articles of clothing and nursery rhymes which serve the same function, that of giving comfort. Without a richly populated intermediate space the child has no shock absorbers, but if the environment is rich with sources of parental love then the child is likely to be more adventurous, creative, and confident.

God may become an object of intermediate space, since God is not entirely a product of the child's own imagination and yet is charged with the emotional associations of powerful and intimate human relationships, especially the parents, grandparents, and older brothers and sisters. The use of personal pronouns such as he or she to describe God, stories about God's activities, and the practice of speaking with God in prayer, help the child to create God as an invisible friend. This may be enriched by images of God as a baby, as flower or a song, together with the metaphysical attributes of God like omnipresence and eternity. If God is also encountered outside the home, whether in school or church, God can become a mysterious, intriguing, and powerful presence in the life of a young child.

The question is, however, what developmental use will be made of the images and concepts of God. Will God become and remain a genuine transitional object, encouraging movement, flexibility, and adventurous confidence, or will God become a fetish-like word, full of inexpressible, magical power, which will inhibit the child's development and lead to a permanent, uncritical, and infantile faith?

Transitional objects not only occupy the intermediate space between the inner and outer worlds, and offer ways of making progress from simple to more complex forms of behavior, they also offer solace in the passage from waking to sleeping life. It is when the child is about to surrender to sleep, to become vulnerable to dreams which may be frightening and to loneliness that objects are needed which will ease the passage. This is why the going-to-bed rituals are so significant to young children. The special blanket must be found, and if the favorite soft toy is lost the child will not go to bed. There is a routine of tucking-in, of final stories, then the goodnight kiss, while the child calls out "Come and see if I'm asleep," thus establishing a final security against being alone and helpless in the night hours. It is now that the child may suck his or her fingers, twist a lock of hair, or insist upon holding the ear of a favorite doll. Many children will now croon snatches of songs, or chant "mummy" in a sing-song way until overtaken by sleep. Against this background, we must discuss the significance of prayers and Bible stories when they form part of this passage from consciousness to unconsciousness.

Faith or Fetish?

If the child aged four goes happily to school clutching his toy rabbit, we may speak of a healthy and creative use of a transitional object, but if at the age of 30 the adult cannot make a speech or attend an interview without secretly caressing the tattered ear of the same toy rabbit, now tied around his waist, we are dealing with a fetish. The child becomes more independent through use of the transitional object; the adult has become dependent upon it. Transitional objects are ephemeral; the corner of the blanket passes away and is replaced by the teddy bear, which in turn becomes the marble set or the motorbike.

The fetish-like object remains fixed and unchangeable, and becomes the object of irrational fears if it is lost, and the source of intense emotions if it is touched. The fetish pulls the adult back to the security of a long past childhood, while the genuine transitional object calls the child onward to a creative adulthood.

The creative transitional object may become a fetish when it has not been chosen by the child, and is not available for the child's own creative re-composition. If when the child is ready to lose interest in the toy, the parent continually re-presents it to the child, discouraging the child's attempt to go beyond it, the result may well become a fetish-like adherence. The genuinely transitional object serves the child's interests, but the fetish-like object serves the interests of the parents. The sensible parent provides a stimulating environment in which there are plenty of opportunities for the choice of transitional object, but lets the child choose, encourages elaboration and fanciful play, and allows the object to evolve. If the object is withheld from the child as a punishment, or used as a bribe, or if the parent regards the child's use of the object as a mark of the child's apparent loyalty and love, then the object may well become a fetish. "Where is the little elephant I gave you for your birthday? Don't you play with it any more?" The aggrieved tone, the hurt voice, and the implied threat all suggest blame and guilt, and encourage the child to cling to the object for the wrong reasons.

The nurture of the child's faith should always be conducted with a certain lightness of touch. Let us suppose a young child is refusing to come upstairs to bed. If you pick the child up physically and carry it upstairs, you will have a kicking, screaming child. If you command the child to hold your hand, and then lead the child upstairs, not holding the child's hand but reminding the child again and again to hold your hand, the child will perhaps whimper a bit but will stop screaming. The child has been persuaded to take an initiative, to hold your hand. To be commanded and to obey involves an inward act of agreement, but to be forced against your will is an insult and an indignity.

I am certainly not suggesting that we should command children to pray, and expect their obedience. I am suggesting that the child should always be able to take an initiative, should have the freedom to change the contract, and that we should not, whether through psychological or physical means, establish a situation in which the child complies without any inner assent. Mere compliance will lead to falsehood, to the fetish-like faith. The child should not be allowed to have the last word, nor should the parent immediately capitulate to negativism. The context of nurture should always be negotiation.

The parent should ask the child, "Would you like to say a prayer?" If the answer is no, the answer should be accepted and respected. "Would you like to listen while I say a prayer?" is a question to which many children will say yes, having said no to the first question. "Would you like to say a prayer after me if I say it first?" "Have you learned any new prayers lately?" are additional variants, but the point should not be pressed.

Example 34

PARENT:	Would you like to say the Lord's Prayer?
CHILD (aged 4.2):	Yes.
PARENT:	Say after me then: Our Father
CHILD:	Our Father
PARENT:	Which art in heaven
CHILD:	(*No reply*)
PARENT:	Which art in heaven?
CHILD:	(Child's name) doesn't know which are in heaven.
PARENT:	OK. Miss that bit out then. Hallowed be Thy name.
CHILD:	(No comment)
PARENT:	Hallowed be Thy name?
CHILD:	(Child's name) doesn't know hallowed be Thy name.
PARENT:	OK. Thy kingdom come.
CHILD:	(Child's name) doesn't know that bit.
PARENT:	OK.
CHILD:	Daddy (child's name) knows Our Father, Amen.

PARENT: (*placing hand on child's head*) O.K. That's
            fine. Our Father, Amen.

Often it is best to let children take the initiative in request-
ing prayer. Sometimes this will come from church or school.
Individual styles will, of course, vary widely from one religious
tradition to another, but I have always found it best to avoid the
"God bless mummy and daddy" pattern. In general children
should not be encouraged to offer petitions in prayer, since this
easily establishes a magical aura around prayer, feeds the
child's fantasies of omnipotence, and establishes God as being
a magical giver of all bounties, leading inevitably to disappoint-
ment and rationalization. It is far more creative to encourage the
child to express gratitude; it is better to be thankful for what has
happened than to lay out magical words against fear. The use of
memorized liturgical prayers is often the most satisfactory. If
the child is taught the Lord's Prayer, there are endless opportunities for conversation and reflection. The child will understand the words, since they will be in the context of a trusted
relationship at the close of the day. They will be enjoyed for their
sound and their familiarity, while as conversational gambits
they can gradually be extended so as to create networks of
meaning. It does not matter that a child cannot all at once offer
an adult understanding of a prayer. The great liturgical prayers,
whether it is "lighten our darkness" or "Hail Mary, full of grace"
offer the child a rich religious vocabulary and an opportunity for
image-formation. It does not matter if there are weeks or
months when there is no prayer. The presence of God can be
realized in many ways, and the child must not be conditioned
into believing that the passage from wakefulness to sleep is
dangerous or sinful unless accompanied by prayer. This turns
prayer into a talisman against the dark. Whether we wake or
sleep, we are the Lord's, and whether we pray or not his presence
is with us. Prayer can be the realization of that presence, but
only if it is entered into creatively and flexibly.

Prayer can often be introduced in the context of ordinary
conversation. The typical final conversations of the day often
involve laughter over something which happened, recollection

62

of a happiness, and anticipation of something which will take place tomorrow, or a shared memory. In these little exchanges, when the child has the parent all alone, there is a first encounter with self-criticism, with life-review, and with the selective evaluation of the day. "What is worth remembering? What is worth looking forward to?" This is the unspoken agenda of these last conversations. God as the participant in these conversations is the natural bond of sympathy and of value. The God whom we present to our children in Christian nurture must, however, always be the God who calls our children up out of the house of bondage, out of slavery into freedom. Let us therefore give our children a rich repertoire of symbols which will enhance their creativity and which will lead them into a lifetime of security and risk-taking, but let us not inflict upon them rigid patterns of obligation charged with magical hopes and guilty fears.

We shall conclude this chapter by taking a few examples from conversation about the Bible.

The Bible and Young Children

Almost all the narrative material in the Bible is suitable for use with young children especially in the domestic context, where there is plenty of time for discussion and where themes of a story can be returned to again and again. There are certainly some stories, and parts of stories, which involve such adult passions (the rape of Tamar by her brother) or such horrific violence (killing a sleeping man by banging a nail through his forehead with a hammer) that it is doubtful if the most adventurous parent would feel entirely comfortable about using them, especially at bedtime. Nevertheless, in general parents have been too nervous about the emotional problems of Biblical stories and too cautious about adapting the stories to the child's level of understanding. Many of the most "unsuitable" stories give rise to discussions which are central to the child's interests. Most young children will not understand that the reason why King David tried so hard to persuade Uriah the Hittite to spend a night with his wife Bathsheba was so that people would think the father of Bathsheba's child soon to be born was Uriah not David. This involves a knowledge of the role of the father in conception, of the delay between conception and birth, and of the possibility of creating a false impression about the true biological father of a child. Nevertheless the broad outlines of this story are well within the grasp of most young children: you love someone, and you want to get rid of your rival by having him killed. This emotional triangle springs directly out of the world of the child aged four or five and can be immensely fascinating for such a child.

Much more damage is likely to be caused by the miracle stories in the Bible. These can easily create a fairy tale atmosphere of wish fulfillment and can pander to ideas of grandiosity and omnipotence in the young child. The passionate realism of the stories of human character and motive are far preferable to the incomprehensible and alienating stories of other-worldly wonders.

Example 35

CHILD (aged 6): (*after listening to story of miracle by Jesus*) Why is it so hard to be a Christian today?

PARENT: What makes you say it is hard?

CHILD: Well, so many things happened in those days that don't seem to happen any longer.

PARENT: It's even harder than you think. There are lots and lots of people today who aren't Christians at all.

CHILD: Wow! Who are they?

PARENT: Well, there was once a wonderful man called Muhammad who taught people about God, and lots of people today follow him. They are called Muslims.

Interpretation

The parent might, of course, have maintained that the Bible stories (the child was thinking of the miracles) do continue to happen today. The problem with this response is that it commits the parent to the defense of a literal interpretation of the Biblical miracles, and it prevents the child from entering into a critical relationship with the Bible. It is often better to accept the difficulty which a child points out, and to explore it from within, rather than contradicting it.

Such contradiction can lead the child directly into the conflicts between faith and reason, with magic on one side and real life on the other, or with the submission of the will placed against development of the character.

Example 36

The father had just finished telling a Biblical miracle story to a three-year-old. The older child was listening.

OLDER CHILD (aged 8):	We've done miracles at school.
PARENT:	Oh. So you know what a miracle is.
CHILD:	Yes. A miracle is something impossible that happened.
PARENT:	If it's impossible, how could it happen?
CHILD:	God made it happen.
PARENT:	So it wasn't really impossible.
CHILD:	(doubtfully) No.
PARENT:	Really impossible things can't happen, can they? If they do happen, that proves they weren't really impossible.
CHILD:	Yes, but that's what the teacher said.

Interpretation

Self-contradictory ideas do not become comprehensible just by adding God. It is not a good idea to commit a child to belief in a self-contradictory statement on authority. Authority itself either loses credibility or becomes mystifying and absolute. How should questions about the Bible and truth be dealt with in conversation with young children?

Even children of three and four may ask about the truth of a story, although such enquiries are more common from children aged five and six. In general, the response of the parent and teacher to such questions should be the same for the five-year-old as for the 15-year-old. It is not true that children can ask a question but be incapable of understanding the answer. No child asks a question without experiencing a difficulty or having been challenged by a problem. The adult must enter into conversation, but this does not always mean offering an answer. It is usually more important to understand the question, and it is often here that the adult goes wrong. A long answer is provided dealing with an angle which was, perhaps, not on the child's mind, and the child loses interest.

Many parents are overburdened by the responsibility of representing orthodoxy, as they imagine it, and feel unable to enter into conversation with their own children. This is a great pity, since the important and satisfying thing for the child is often the conversation itself. The difficulty can be explored and recognized, even if no definite conclusion is arrived at.

Example 37

(a) PARENT: So who were Adam and Eve really?
CHILD (aged 7):   Well, they were sort of the first people, but they are also everybody. Adam is all the men and Eve is all the women.
PARENT: (*surprised*) Who told you that?
CHILD: (*triumphantly*) I've got a thinking machine inside my head, you know!

(b) CHILD: What happened next?
PARENT: Well, in one story . . . but there's another story which says . . .

CHILD: Which is right?

PARENT: I don't know. But the main point is . . .

(c) CHILD: Is that true?

PARENT: Well, it's true'ish.

CHILD: What is true'ish?

PARENT: It means when people have loved a story for a long, long time and have told it lots of times until nobody really knows any longer what really happened, so we say its true'ish.

CHILD: It's sort of true?

(d) PARENT: (*telling the story of Balaam's ass*) Now here we come to a part of the story that is rather strange. I'm going to tell it to you just the way people have always told it and you can see what you think about it.

CHILDREN: What happened?

PARENT Well, all of a sudden the donkey spoke. It said "Why are you hitting me?" Haven't I been your faithful donkey all these years?

CHILDREN: (*laughing*) It didn't!

PARENT: Well, that's what the story says so you can take it or leave it. Do you want me to go on with the story?

CHILDREN: (*eagerly*) Yes.

PARENT: Well, the story goes on to say that when Balaam heard his ass talking . . .

Interpretation

These discussions illustrate some of the ways in which children may be helped to relate to sacred stories in a way which does not stifle imagination and inquiry. The idea that a story has more than one version comes easily to children, especially if they are used to variations in other well-loved stories. There are, for example, many versions of the traditional story about Little Red Riding Hood. Telling the story from the point of view of first this character and then that is another way of helping children to see that stories are different when told by different people and seen through other people's experience. Children should not be introduced to the Bible stories in isolation, but as part of a larger world of story. Stories of the ancient Greek gods and goddesses are beautiful, rich with cultural associations, and full of human and religious power. Great secular epics such as the *Iliad,* the *Odyssey,* and *The Lord of the Rings* have an importance in creating an enjoyment of narrative and in introducing many universal symbols.

Stories should not be confined to the great epics and to sacred literature. The spontaneously composed stories which parents tell to their children are just as important. Children love stories about their toys and dolls, about their known relatives and their great-great-grandparents. The story world of the child radiates out from the question "What happened today?" The horizon of the child's own life is measured in anecdote, and this ultimately merges with the horizons of the people of the Bible, and with the story of all humanity.

V

THE STRUCTURE OF RELIGIOUS CONVERSATION

Jesus taught through conversation. He also taught through parables, actions, and sermons. But if we asked how he taught the woman at the well, Nicodemus and the woman from Syro-Phoenicia, the answer is clear: it was through conversation. Some interesting progress is being made today in understanding how conversation enables children and young people to develop morally, socially, and religiously. What seems to matter is not only the subject of conversation, but the manner. In other words, it matters how the conversation is conducted.

Conversation Stage by Stage

As they grow in their capacities for thinking and feeling, children seem to pass through a number of stages or patterns. When a pattern begins to break up, it is restructured within a new pattern, which includes the old one at a higher level. An element (like belief in God) can be included in the patterns of all the stages, but what it means to have faith in God will differ from one pattern to the next. We can summarize this point by saying that the content (belief in God) may be fairly consistent but the structure or pattern (the manner of believing) undergoes important changes.

Since the middle 1970s some teachers have been learning how to talk with children so as to match their stage of development. A stage is a pattern of thinking and responding, and a

69

conversation also has a manner, a style, or a structure, quite apart from the actual subject of the conversation. It is possible to match the pattern of conversation with the pattern of thinking or feeling, or to pitch the conversation just above the stage where the children are. Teachers found that by doing this, it was possible to advance the structure of the children's thinking. This technique can be called "conversational intervention."

Before the development of conversation really starts, we can describe a very early period which can be called "pre-argumentation." There is little or no interest in understanding the other person's point of view. Subjects of conversation are changed abruptly, or the same thing is simply repeated again and again. Arguments are won by endurance or by brute force.

The first real stage of conversation can be called "single-reason argumentation." At this stage, it is recognized that it is necessary to convince the opponent, but thinking is not sufficiently mature to produce real reasons. The reasons are thought up afterwards, to defend a position which has been adopted more or less on the spur of the moment. This passes into the second stage, which can be called the stage of "maintaining connections." Now the interest begins to move away from who is right to what is right. The argument is now seen to be a joint enterprise to which each partner is contributing. One reason can now follow another reason, i.e., reasons are given for reasons. People notice similarities between each other's points of view and try to avoid direct confrontation.

"Counter-evidence" is the name which can be given to stage three. At this stage, logical and conversational abilities have developed to the point where contradictions can be spotted, both in one's own position and in that of the partner. The strength of an argument now tends to be tested by its ability to withstand refutation. One can reason about the patterns of reasoning displayed by the opponent. Weak or irrelevant arguments can now be dropped, and distinctions are made between facts and values, e.g., this is what she did, but what should she have done? Although there is now much more interest in the argument itself, traces of personal power rather than interest in truth seeking still survive.

"Shared analysis" is the name sometimes given to the fourth stage. For the first time, we have genuine dialogue, a mutual sharing in conversation. The purpose of the conversation is to discover, understand, and apply a shared or common meaning. Now the partners think up reasons in support of each other's positions, not just their own. Degrees of probability are assessed and conclusions are sometimes only tentative. General moral and social rules are used to test conclusions, test cases are examined, and there is the ability to distinguish premises from conclusions.

Finally, we come to stage five, "ideal discourse." It is now recognized that everybody taking part in the conversation is under an obligation to struggle for the most just solution to the problem. Nobody should be excluded and the weight of the argument alone rather than the weight of authority or personality is considered. It is now recognized that there are different kinds of argument which call upon different kinds of evidence. Universal principles of truth, validity, and human rights are recognized and acted upon. It is understood that each participant needs the other, and that the contribution of each one is liable to error and fallibility. Individual conflict now disappears as the community searches for the truth. While the order of these patterns is probably predictable, the age at which any person will enter each type of pattern will vary considerably. In general, "pre-argumentation" is typical of early childhood, stage 1 ("single-reason argumentation") middle childhood, and stage 2 ("maintaining connections") is typical of late childhood or pre-adolescence. Stage 3 ("counter-evidence") is often found in adolescence although signs of it may appear earlier. Whether stage 3 will be left behind will depend upon many factors including both individual and cultural ones. Stages 4 and 5 are adult stages, the latter being quite rare. Features of earlier stages may reappear under stress as any listener to broadcasts from the Houses of Parliament will notice.

Conversation and Religious Maturity

We have been looking at a brief summary of stages of conversational growth. These are expressions of the way people share in a search for the truth, and talk with each other as part of that search. Children, young people, and adults will pass through these different kinds of pattern as they grow in maturity, and God will be patterned in conversation in accordance with these different stages. In other words, conversational patterns about God enable him to be approached and understood in these different ways.

Conversational intervention could become an important technique for the teacher and the parent. Each stage or pattern of conversational type has to be broken down into its separate features, so that the teacher can introduce features typical of the next highest stage. It would be possible to apply these conversational patterns to Bible stories, so that a story was not just told, but was interrupted by and followed by conversational interventions which would engage the children at the appropriate level.

BACKGROUND READING

For the use of anecdotal material in child observation research see Philip T. Slee, *Child Observation Skills,* London, Croom Helm, 1987, pp. 35-37. Other studies of the religious conversations of children include Violet Madge, *Children in Search of Meaning,* London, SCM Press, 1965, and *Introducing Young Children to Jesus,* London, SCM Press, 1971, and Christopher Herbert, *Listening to Children: A Fresh Approach to Religious Education in the Primary Years,* Church Information Office for General Synod Board of Education, 1983. For accounts of more systematic interviews with children involving religious conversation, see Ronald Goldman, *Religious Thinking from Childhood to Adolescence,* Routledge & Kegan Paul, 1964, and David Heller, *The Children's God,* University of Chicago Press, 1986. Kenneth Hyde's comprehensive review of the research on religion in childhood will be published by the Religious Education Press, Birmingham, Alabama, in 1990 under the title *Religion in Childhood and Adolescence: A Review of the Research.*

Chapter One

The background to Chapter One is provided by the work of Jean Piaget. In *The Child and Reality,* Viking Press, 1974, he emphasizes that intelligence precedes language, and that the bridge from sensori-motor schemes of intelligence to concrete operational thought is provided by images or configurations. This "pictorial intelligence" is the principal feature of the thinking of the child between ages two and seven and is the basis of the distinction made in this book between pictorial thinking about God and propositional thinking about God.

My first criticisms of the unfortunate effect of ignoring images in the religious education of young children appeared as the editorial of the *British Journal of Religious Education*, Vol. 8, No. 2, Spring 1986, pp. 59-61, under the title "The Religious Education of the Younger Child." The section "God-Talk with Children" (pp. 60f.) is the seed from which the present set of notes has developed. These ideas form the basis of the "Religious Education in the Early Years" project which will be described in a later publication.

An account of the philosophical thinking-skills of young children is provided by Matthew Lipman, et al., *Philosophy in the Classroom*, Philadelphia, Temple University Press, 1980.

On God as both abstract and concrete see the various studies by Charles Hartshorne, and the discussion in Ralph E. James, *The Concrete God: A New Beginning for Theology: The Thought of Charles Hartshorne*, New York, Bobbs-Merrill, 1967.

On the role of the imagination see Maria Harris, *Teaching and Religious Imagination*, San Francisco, Harper and Row, 1987, and Kieran Egan and Dan Nadener (eds.), *Imagination and Education*, Open University Press, 1988, especially the article by Robin Barrow, "Some Observations on the Concept of Imagination," pp. 79-90.

The faith development theory of James W. Fowler and his associates has important insights to offer on the power of images to give structure to human growth. See James W. Fowler, *Stages of Faith*, San Francisco, Harper and Row, 1981.

Chapter Two

For discussion of the imagery of God see Gordon D. Kaufman, *The Theological Imagination: Constructing the Concept of God*, London, SCM Press, 1983, Philip Wheelwright, *The Burning Fountain: A Study in the Language of Symbolism*, Gloucester, Peter Smith, 1982, and Sallie McFague, *Metaphorical Theology: Models of God in Religious Language*, London, SCM Press, 1983.

The role of imagery in teaching about God is discussed by Gloria Durka and Joanmarie Smith, *Modelling God,* Mahwah, N.J., Paulist Press, 1976, Andrew Mcgrady, "A Metaphor and Model Paradigm of Religious Thinking," *British Journal of Religious Education,* Vol. 9, No. 2, Spring 1987, pp. 84-94, and Kathryn F. Raban, "Guided Imagery, Young Children and Religious Education," *British Journal of Religious Education,* Vol. 10, No. 1, Autumn 1987, pp. 15-22.

Chapter Three

The most powerful attempt to understand how the thinking of young children about justice develops is to be found in the work of Lawrence Kohlberg. The psychological essays are gathered in a single volume: Lawrence Kohlberg, *The Psychology of Moral Development (Essays on Moral Development Vol. 2).* New York, Harper and Row, 1984. A review of the current research into the relationship between the moral and religious thinking of children and young people is provided by Fritz Oser and K. H. Reich, "Moral Judgement, Religious Judgement and Logical Thought: A Review of their Relationship," *British Journal of Religious Education* Vol. 12, No.2, Spring 1990, (pp. 99-101) and No. 3, Summer 1990 (pp. 172-181).

Since the late 1970s the Swiss psychologist Fritz Oser has been publishing studies of the development of children's thinking about God. The relationship between the child and God is seen as part of the development of the child's interpretation of the world as a whole. Oser's work throws light on prayer, miracle, and revelation as these are interpreted by children. See Fritz Oser, "Stages of Religious Judgement" in Christiane Brusselmans (ed.), *Toward Moral and Religious Maturity,* Morristown, N.J., Silver Burdett Company, 1980, pp. 277-315.

The discussions of children's conversations in the present study are influenced not only by cognitive stage developmental theory, especially Fowler and Oser, but also by interpretation theory. The idea that experience of God is mediated by the grammatical structure of the speech or writing through which

God is encountered is taken from the article by Paul Ricoeur, "Toward a Hermeneutic of Revelation" in his *Essays on Biblical Interpretation*, SPCK, 1981, pp. 73-118.

For discussion about the place of the Bible in the religious development of children see Jack Priestley, "Religious Story and the Literary Imagination," *British Journal of Religious Education*, Vol. 3, No. 3, Summer 1981, pp. 17-24 and the reply by John Bailey in Vol. 4, No. 3, Summer 1982, pp. 152-55, together with the articles by J. E. Greer, Andrew McGrady, and Nicola Slee in *Can We Teach the Bible? British Journal of Religious Education* (Special Issue), Vol. 5, No. 3, Summer 1983.

Chapter Four

An important influence on the interpretations offered in this study about the place of religious conversation in the lives of young children is that of psychoanalytic object-relations theory. Religious language is structured by cognitive development but it is driven by the emotional context of early family life. The main source for the idea of "intermediate space" used in this chapter is Donald W. Winnicott, *Playing and Reality*, New York, Tavistock Publications, 1971, together with his two collections of essays, *Through Paediatrics to Psychoanalysis*, New York, Basic Books, 1958, and *The Maturational Process and the Facilitating Environment*, New York, International Universities Press, 1965. Although not concerned with the religious aspects, Simon A. Grolnick and Leonard Barkin (eds.), *Between Reality and Fantasy*, New York, Jason Aronson Inc., 1978, is a valuable collection of studies. The application of object-relations theory to religious life is best studied in John McDargh, *Psychoanalytic Object-Relations Theory and the Study of Religion: On Faith and the Imagery of God*, New York, University Press of America, 1983, and Paul C. Horton, *Solace: The Missing Dimension in Psychiatry*, University of Chicago Press, 1981.

The reflections about the origins of a fetish-like commitment were inspired by Robert Dickes, "Parents, Transitional Objects and Childhood Fetishes," Chapter 20, in the Grolnick and Barkin symposium, *op. cit.* In the same collection Chapter 16 by Joseph C. Solomon, "Transitional Phenomena and Obsessive Compulsive States" throws interesting light upon stereotyped ritual behavior in adult life. The influence of mothering and fathering upon the religious lives of children and on the adults they will someday become is discussed in Philip M. Helfaer, *The Psychology of Religious Doubt,* Boston, Beacon Press, 1972, Anamaria Rizzuto, *The Birth of the Living God,* University of Chicago Press, 1979, and W. W. Meissner, *Psychoanalysis and Religious Experience,* Yale University Press, 1984.

I have discussed the significance of the critical dimension in religious education and Christian nurture in "Christian Nurture and Critical Openness," *Studies in Religion and Education,* Falmer Press, 1984, pp. 207-226, *World Religions for Christian Children* (Presidential Address), Redhill, Surrey, National Christian Education Council, 1985, and "Authority and Freedom in Religious Education" in Brian Gates (ed.), *SHAP Working Party, 20th Anniversary Volume,* Collins. For an application to teaching the Bible see my *The Bible in the Secular Classroom* (St Hild and St Bede Lecture) North of England Institute of Christian Education, 1986.

Chapter Five

This chapter is adapted from my short article "The Role of Conversation in Christian Education," *Education in Church Today,* No. 1, Spring 1989, pp. 5-9 which was in turn based on Marvin W. Berkolwitz, Fritz Oser, and M. L. Berkowitz and Wolfgang Althof, "The Development of Sociomoral Discourse" in Williams M. Kurtins and Jakob L. Gewirtz (eds.), *Moral Development Through Social Interaction,* New York, Wiley and Sons, 1987, pp. 322-352. On the characteristics of the stages of conversation see M. W. Berkowitz and J. C. Gibbs, "Measuring the Developmental Features of Moral Discussion," *Merrill-Palmer Quarterly,* Vol. 29, 1983, pp. 399-410.

DATE DUE

MAR 2 5 1994			
NOV 7 '95 NOV 2 1 2002			
APR 0 1 2003			
MAY 2 1 2003			